inspirations

FRESH FLOWERS

Over 20 imaginative arrangements for the home

inspirations

FRESH FLOWERS

Over 20 imaginative arrangements for the home

GILLY LOVE

PHOTOGRAPHY BY MICHELLE GARRETT

LORENZ BOOKS

This edition first published in 1998 by Lorenz Books

27 West 20th Street

New York, NY 10011

LORENZ BOOKS are available for bulk purchase for sales
promotion and for premium use. For details, write or call the sales
director, Lorenz Books, 27 West 20th Street, New York, NY 10011; (800) 354-9657

Lorenz Books is an imprint of
Anness Publishing Limited

ISBN 1 85967 607 3

Publisher: Joanna Lorenz
Senior Editor: Alison Macfarlane
Designer: Simon Wilder
Photographer: Michelle Garrett
Stylists: Michelle Garrett and Gilly Love

Printed in Hong Kong / China

3 5 7 9 10 8 6 4 2

CONTENTS

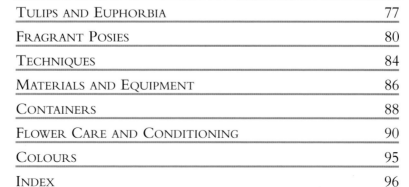

INTRODUCTION	6
SCENTED FLOWERPOT	8
SEASIDE FLOWERS	12
SUMMER VEGETABLE VASES	16
HOT AND SPICY EDIBLE FLOWERS	20
CELEBRATION ROSES AND HERBS	23
WREATH WITH FLOATING CANDLES	26
THREE-TIER TOPIARY TREE	29
TRANSLUCENT FLOWERS	32
SCENTED *POT-ET-FLEUR*	36
ROSE PYRAMID	40
HERB AND DRIED FRUITS WREATH	44
ROMANTIC BEDSIDE POSY	47
AL FRESCO FRUIT VASES	50
TRADITIONAL BOUQUET	54
EXOTIC FLOWERS	57
GOLDEN WALNUT POTS	60
AROMATIC CHRISTMAS WREATH	64
FLOWER EGGS	67
SPRING FLOWER BASKET	70
SPRING FLOWERS	74
TULIPS AND EUPHORBIA	77
FRAGRANT POSIES	80
TECHNIQUES	84
MATERIALS AND EQUIPMENT	86
CONTAINERS	88
FLOWER CARE AND CONDITIONING	90
COLOURS	95
INDEX	96

INTRODUCTION

A BUNCH OF FRESHLY picked and personally chosen flowers is a joy to receive and a pleasure to give. Every single flower is unique and no arrangement or bouquet can ever or should ever be exactly repeated – that is what makes a gift of flowers so individual and special. As a child I would go along with my mother, who is a keen flower arranger, to numerous demonstrations and competitions, even helping out at church festivals, but at home I do little more than buy flowers and put them straight into a vase.

This book is just what I need to make me more creative and I hope it will do the same for you. The projects are a mix of simple arrangements and more formal designs for special events, each illustrated step by step and with easy-to-follow instructions. There are ideas for every room and occasion. There are flowers for the bathroom and for bedside tables; flowers for contemporary homes and for more traditional interiors; and flowers for presents and for tablesettings. There are projects that include preparing your own containers and tips to make just a few flowers look like a massive display.

All of the projects are really simple and should only take a few minutes to make. You don't need a year of evening classes to master the techniques, and you don't need to spend a fortune on expensive materials either. The cost of fresh flowers, of course, varies from season to season, so be flexible and choose varieties that are in peak condition and plentiful. If you can't find one of the flowers in one of the arrangements featured here, select another that is similar. Above all, be kind to your flowers, giving them the proper care, and they will reward you with days and sometimes weeks of fresh and natural beauty.

Deborah Barker

SCENTED FLOWERPOT

Pink is a romantic and feminine colour; it creates a relaxing and joyful atmosphere in bathrooms. Bright pink 'Stargazer' lilies have an intoxicating perfume, enhanced here by adding a few drops of an essential oil such as geranium or sweet orange to the bath salts.

YOU WILL NEED
small jar or glass
glass flowerpot
uncoloured bath salts
plastic bag
pink food colouring
funnel
pink bath beads
small shells
geranium or sweet orange essential oil
jug
flower food
'Stargazer' lilies
scissors or sharp knife
sweet peas
gloriosa
poppies

1 Place the small jar or glass inside the flowerpot. (You need a jar that will leave a space of about 2.5 cm/1 in between it and the pot.) Put the bath salts in a sturdy plastic bag and add a couple of drops of food colouring.

2 Shake well until the salts have acquired a uniform colour. Add more colouring if necessary until you have the colour you want.

3 Using a funnel, pour the bath salts into the flower-pot, filling the space between the containers to just below the rim of the inner pot.

8

4 Add pink bath beads and small shells to create a border on top of the salts. Add a few drops of essential oil to the bath salts.

5 Using the funnel, carefully fill the inner container with water and flower food, taking care not to splash the bath salts.

6 Strip the lower leaves from the 'Stargazer' lilies and cut to a length approximately twice the height of the flowerpot. Arrange the lilies in the pot.

7 The pollen stamens can stain clothing and the petals of the flowers: to avoid this snip them off using a pair of scissors. ▶

8 Add the sweet peas, turning the arrangement around as you do so to build up a regular shape.

9 Insert two or three heads of gloriosa to add a darker contrasting colour to the arrangement.

10 Add the poppies last, being careful not to bruise their petals, which damage very easily. Rotate the arrangement and fill any remaining gaps.

Right: The colour of the bath salts can be altered to complement the colour of the flowers; the pink here brings out the pink of the lilies.

SEASIDE FLOWERS

Mussels are available for the most of the year and provide a constant source of pretty shells that can be used to fill the insides of transparent glass vases or as an attractive mulch on the topsoil of pot plants. Here, they are applied to the sides of a terracotta pot to make a decorative border.

YOU WILL NEED
12 mussels
knife
scrubbing brush
square-sided terracotta pot
rubber gloves
sea-blue emulsion paint
paintbrush
glue gun and glue sticks
clear nail varnish
small jam jar
plastic or florist's foam
jug
flower food
eryngium (sea holly)
scabious
blue cornflowers
nigella (love-in-a-mist)

1 Remove the mussels from the shells and scrub the shells thoroughly. Any remaining flesh should flake off quite easily once they are completely dry. Check each one as even the tiniest piece will make a rather nasty smell if left attached to the shell.

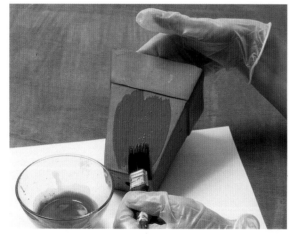

2 Paint the terracotta pot using a weak dilution of blue emulsion paint and water to create a soft, colour-washed effect. Allow to dry thoroughly.

3 Using a glue gun and glue sticks, stick the mussel shells evenly around the rim of the pot.

4 Give each shell a soft gleam by applying a coat of clear nail varnish.

5 Place the jam jar in the pot, wedging it firmly inside using a piece of plastic or some odd scraps of florist's foam, and fill it with water and flower food. Strip any leaves off the eryngium and use it to make the overall shape of the arrangement.

6 Add several stems of scabious, first stripping off any lower leaves.

7 Add the contrasting colour of deep blue cornflowers, again stripping off any lower leaves. ▶

8 Add the nigella: these flowers resemble tiny sea anemones, and the delicate fern-like foliage around each flower's head has the effect of making the arrangement appear more fragile and delicate.

9 Finally, place the remaining mussel shells around the top of the pot to conceal the glass jar.

Right: Blue flowers and sea shells are particularly suited to bathroom arrangements. Keep topping up the flowers for a permanent display of colour, taking out the dead ones and adding new.

SUMMER VEGETABLE VASES

Many vegetables add a decorative surface to simple, straight-sided vases: halved courgettes (zucchini), carrots and peppers, okra or whole runner beans (string beans) and mangetout (snow peas). The vegetables should echo the food you are planning to serve.

YOU WILL NEED
3 straight-sided vases of different sizes
double-sided tape
flat green beans
sharp knife
fine stems of asparagus
natural raffia
jug
flower food
green-flowered moluccella
white delphiniums
thin canes
scissors or sharp knife
horsemint (*Mentha longifolia*)
variegated lemon balm
alpine strawberry
astrantia

1 Choose 3 or more vases, depending on the size of your dining table. Provided they are all straight-sided they may be of different styles as, once covered, they will have a harmonious appearance.

2 Make sure each glass vessel is completely dust-free and dry. Take the largest vase and add two rows of double-sided tape, as in the picture.

3 Turn the vase on its side and press similar-sized flat beans – the flatter the better – on to the double-sided-tape. Align the ends of the beans just over the rim of the vase and trim the stalk ends at the bottom with a sharp knife. Cover all four sides.

4 Repeat the process with the smaller vases, which may need only one strip of double-sided tape. Press the asparagus firmly on to the sides, with the tips pointing upwards. Trim the stalks as before.

5 Tie raffia around the centre of the vases, both for decoration and to make sure the vegetables stay firmly in place.

6 Fill the vases with water and flower food.

7 Starting with the larger vase, create an overall shape using green-flowered moluccella.

8 Delphiniums tend to be rather top-heavy and are prone to keeling over, but their stems are quickly given some additional support by inserting a thin cane. This does no harm to the flower, which can still take up water, but it keeps the stem rigid and strong. ▶

9 Add the delphiniums to the arrangement. Strip off and reserve any flower heads that are too low on the stem, cutting them off as close to the stalk as possible.

10 To give the arrangement a faint scent that will harmonize with food but will not overpower it, add a few stems of relaxing horsemint. Turn the vase around to ensure it has a balanced and even arrangement of flowers on all sides.

11 Variegated lemon balm creates the leafy framework for the small vases. Like mint, it aids digestion and is both relaxing and rejuvenating.

12 Add stems of alpine strawberry on which the flowers and the immature fruits occur on the same fine stalk. Tiny pink astrantia flowers blend with the pinky tips of the asparagus.

13 Finally, gently insert the reserved delphinium flower heads and rotate the vase to make sure it is balanced on all sides.

HOT AND SPICY EDIBLE FLOWERS

Meals featuring aromatic curries or Mexican salsas demand bright, colourful table centres with vibrant flowers and complementary containers. Wide-mouthed drinking glasses are the perfect height and a raft of raffia-bound cinnamon sticks or twigs will support any large flower heads.

YOU WILL NEED
small straight twigs
cinnamon sticks
secateurs (pruners)
natural raffia
scissors or sharp knife
coloured glasses
jug
flower food
courgette (zucchini) flowers
calendulas (pot marigolds)
garden roses
selection of other edible flowers: violas, rocket
flowers, pelargoniums and nasturtiums

1 Cut the twigs and cinnamon sticks with secateurs (pruners) so that they are the right length to rest neatly on the rims of the containers.

2 Tie a strand of raffia to one end of a cinnamon stick. Lay another cinnamon stick at a 60° angle to the first and bind the raffia around both sticks to tie them firmly together, making a triangle. Trim the ends of the raffia. Repeat the process with a third stick to make a triangular raft. Use the same method with four cinnamon sticks or twigs to make a square raft. In this way, make a raft for each container.

3 Fill the selected coloured glasses with fresh water and flower food. ▶

4 Place the prepared rafts on top of the glasses and adjust the raffia ties, if necessary, until they lie flat.

5 Arrange the courgette (zucchini) flowers first. You can use them without the fruit attached, but they do give the flower heads more stability if left on.

6 Add the calendulas (pot marigolds). Calendula petals can also be sprinkled over salads and make a useful substitute for saffron to colour and flavour rice.

7 Choose roses in a hot, bright colour. If you are using the petals to decorate food make sure they come from organically-grown garden roses: florists' flowers may have been sprayed with a post-harvest treatment, making them unsuitable for eating.

8 Fill any gaps with whatever edible flowers you have in the garden or conservatory – violas, rocket flowers, pelargoniums and nasturtiums are all suitable. Many larger supermarkets now sell some edible flowers in their salad departments.

CELEBRATION ROSES AND HERBS

For special meals it is a charming gesture to prepare an individual posy of flowers for each guest, to be taken home as a memento of the occasion. Decorate napkin rings and candlesticks with subtly-toned flowers and herbs and scatter rose petals over the tablecloth just before the meal is served.

YOU WILL NEED
florist's foam
flower food
terracotta pot, preferably old and weathered
kitchen knife
plastic bag or small sheet of plastic
scissors or sharp knife
pointed stick or skewer
selection of herbs: painted sage (*Salvia viridis*),
broad-leaved thyme, rosemary
garden roses
jasmine (*Jasminum officinale*)
handful of carpet moss (sheet moss)

1 Place the florist's foam in water with flower food added until the foam is completely soaked and there are no air bubbles rising from it. Do not leave it any longer or the foam will start to disintegrate. Press the rim of the pot on to the foam and use the indentation as a guide when cutting the foam. It should fit loosely in the pot and come up to just below its rim.

2 Line the pot with the plastic bag or sheet to stop any water leaking. Trim the plastic so that it will be hidden by the flowers.

3 Using a pointed stick or skewer, make 10–15 holes in the foam for the flowers and herbs.

▶

4 Arrange a mixture of herbs in the pot to create a green framework for the flowers. Snip off any leaves that would be embedded in the foam.

5 Once you have a balanced foliage arrangement, place four or five roses in the pot. Snip off the lower leaves and leaf axils. Any larger thorns are best snipped off, too, so that the rose stems go smoothly into the foam without making too large holes.

6 Add a couple of sprays of jasmine flowers to the arrangement for their rich scent.

7 Conceal any visible plastic or foam with a little moss, which will also help to retain the moisture in the foam.

WREATH WITH FLOATING CANDLES

A pretty centrepiece for a buffet table is a shallow dish of floating candles circled with a wreath bursting with brightly coloured flowers and tiny vegetables and fruits. Statice bought as a fresh cut flower will dry very successfully and can be recycled for another occasion.

YOU WILL NEED
florist's foam ring with integral plastic tray
jug
flower food
purple statice
scissors or sharp knife
pointed stick or skewer
stub wires
tindori
wire cutters
yellow habanero chillies
bicoloured carnations
gerbera
zinnia
shallow glass dish to fit inside the wreath
glass pebbles
floating candles

1 Soak the foam ring thoroughly with water with flower food added. Large foam rings are too big to immerse in water unless you put them in the bath but they can be "watered" from a jug. Cut off the statice flowers, leaving about 5 cm/2 in of stem, and use a pointed stick or skewer to make a hole in the foam before inserting each stem. Add flowers to the top and sides of the wreath, leaving spaces for the other flowers, fruit and vegetables.

2 Push a stub wire through the base of each tindori and trim the wire to leave about 5 cm/ 2in sticking out from each side. Gently pull the ends down and twist together to make a rigid "stalk".

3 Push a wire through the base or side of each habanero chilli and cut and twist as for the tindori. (Wash your hands after handling chillies as any juice can be very painful if rubbed near your eyes.) ▶

2 7

4 Cut the stems of the carnations to about 2.5 cm/1 in and make a hole in the foam with the stick or skewer before gently pressing in each stem.

5 Arrange the gerbera in the same way, handling these flowers very gently as they are not as robust as carnations and may snap.

6 Any remaining spaces may be filled with small zinnia flowers, cutting the stems short as for the carnations and gerbera.

7 Fill a shallow glass dish with glass pebbles and floating candles. Arrange it within the wreath on the table and fill it with water.

THREE-TIER TOPIARY TREE

Chrysanthemums are probably the longest-lasting cut flowers, and in a cool place, away from direct sunlight, they can last for several weeks. Lime green 'Shamrock' chrysanthemums, combined with other green flowers, create a sculptural tree shape that complements a modern interior.

YOU WILL NEED
'Hens and Chickens' fresh poppy seed
heads (*Papaver somniferum*)
scissors or sharp knife
natural raffia
square-sided glass vase
glass jar to fit inside vase
jug
flower food
onion seed heads
'Shamrock' chrysanthemums
flat black polished stones
xerophyllum (bear grass)

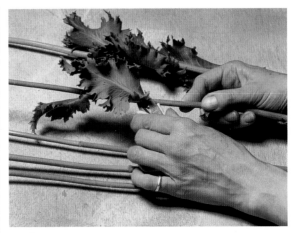

1 Trim all the leaves from the poppy seed heads until you are left with smooth, straight stems.

2 Trim the poppy stems to an equal length, approximately twice the height of the glass vase. Tie the stems firmly together using natural raffia. This binding point will be concealed in the finished flower arrangement.

3 Put a smaller glass jar inside the vase to hold the poppy and onion seed heads firmly together. Fill both the jar and the glass vase with fresh water and flower food. Stand the bunch of poppies in the jar and add the onion seed heads, cutting them about 5 cm/2 in shorter than the poppies.

▶

4 Remove any chrysanthemum leaves that will fall below the water line and trim the stems about 5 cm/2 in shorter than those of the onion seed heads. Arrange the chrysanthemums in the space between the glass jar and the side of the vase.

5 Add enough flat black stones to the vase to conceal the glass jar and the chrysanthemum stems.

6 Take about ten stems of xerophyllum (bear grass) and tie them together about 5 cm/2 in from the bottom with a piece of raffia. Gently bend the stems in half to create a loop and tie in the same place as before.

7 Make another bear grass loop, then gently part the chrysanthemum leaves to tuck the loops into the top of the vase.

TRANSLUCENT FLOWERS

Make the most of just a few flowers by dividing them into several identical posies, each wrapped in a collar of clear cellophane, which then becomes a decorative feature as well as filling out a wide-mouthed vase.

YOU WILL NEED
vase at least half the height of the tallest
flowers
jug
flower food
zantedeschia (arum lilies)
lysimachia (loosestrife)
roses
eustoma
spathiphyllum or hosta leaves
scissors or sharp knife
natural raffia
roll of clear cellophane
clear water-resistant adhesive tape

1 Make sure your chosen vase is completely clean and fill it with water and flower food. Divide the flowers into four or five identical groups, depending on the number of each variety you are using.

2 Remove any of the leaves that will fall below the water line.

3 For comfort while assembling the arrangement, snip off any rose thorns using very sharp scissors.

4 Make a balanced arrangement in your hand, taking one flower from each group.

5 Secure each posy of flowers using a strand of raffia, and tie firmly without crushing any of the stems.

6 Repeat this same process with all the other flowers and leaves.

7 Cut a square of cellophane and fold it in half. In the middle of the crease make a hole big enough for the stems of the flowers to go through.

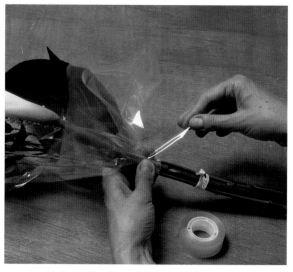

8 Slip a posy in through the hole and fold the edges of the cellophane around the stems so the sides of the square form a loose ruff.

9 Hold the cellophane in position by wrapping a piece of water-resistant adhesive tape around the stems. Wrap all the other posies in cellophane in the same way.

10 Place all the posies in the vase, tweaking the folds of the cellophane to create a continuous collar around the edge of the vase. This arrangement looks especially dramatic when lit from below, so that the translucent cellophane catches the light and shadows from the flowers.

Above: Wrapping flowers in translucent cellophane works with blooms of any colour, but white and cream look very effective in a clear or frosted white glass vase.

SCENTED *POT-ET-FLEUR*

With a few seasonal flowers and some indoor ferns you can create a luscious arrangement known as a pot-et-fleur, *literally translated as "pot and flower". Boston ferns like moist soil and prefer good humidity, which can be improvised by spraying the plants every day with rainwater.*

YOU WILL NEED
basket
plastic sheet
newspaper or packing paper
3–4 pots Boston fern (*Nephrolepis exaltata*)
3–4 jam jars
jug
flower food
peonies
scissors or sharp knife
alpine thistles (*Eryngium alpinum*)
flowering dill (*Anethum graveloens*)
'Blue Bee' delphiniums

1 Line the base of the basket with plastic and fill with newspaper or packing paper to create a level base for the plants and jars. Place a potted fern in the basket and adjust the packing if necessary so that the fronds cascade over the side but the rim of the pot is concealed by the rim of the basket.

2 Add two or three more ferns so that the basket looks well filled but there is enough space inside for the jars that will hold the flowers.

3 Fill the jam jars two-thirds full with water and flower food and wedge firmly between the plant pots, adding more paper if necessary to keep them securely upright.

4 Strip most of the leaves from the peony stems and place one or two stems in each jar. (Large-headed roses could be substituted for the peonies when they are out of season.)

5 Add two or three stems of alpine thistles to each jar after removing all the lower leaves. The thistles are very long-lasting and can be left to dry in the arrangement if you wish.

6 Carefully remove all the lower foliage from the dill as its fern-like leaves will quickly rot and pollute the water.

7 Finally, add some bright blue delphiniums, or you could choose other contrasting flowers such as campanula or purple lupins.

8 Tweak out all the fern fronds so they conceal most of the flower stems, creating the illusion that all the flowers are actually growing in the basket and out of the ferns.

Right: When the fresh flowers die, you can simply take out the jam jars, discard them, and replenish with new ones. You could make a similar arrangement for the table, using a smaller basket without the ferns.

ROSE PYRAMID

Decorative "trees" of tiny spray roses interspersed with hypericum berries would look good at either end of a mantelpiece. These burnt orange and red tones are perfect for autumn, but you might use icy white and cream roses in winter, yellow tones in spring and hot pinks for summer.

YOU WILL NEED
florist's foam
kitchen knife
bucket
flower food
2 flowerpot-shaped containers in
ceramic or metal
spray roses in burnt orange and red
scissors or sharp knife
hypericum berries in light and dark red

1 Before soaking the foam, shave off slivers from the sides using a sharp kitchen knife to form two obelisk shapes. The bottom of each obelisk should fit very snugly into its container.

2 Immerse the foam obelisks in a bucket of water with flower food added and hold them down until all the air bubbles stop rising. Make sure you do not over soak the foam, as it will disintegrate and you will not be able to use it.

3 Press each obelisk into its container until firmly wedged. Shave off a little more foam if necessary to make the obelisks as symmetrical as possible.

4 Carefully remove all the leaves from the rose stems using florist's scissors or a sharp knife.

5 Carefully trim off any thorns so that each rose stem will push smoothly into the foam. Cut the rose stems to a length of about 10 cm/4 in each, depending on the size of the container – the roses need to stick firmly into the foam and just overlap the side of the pot.

6 Cut the berries into similar lengths to the roses, removing any leaves and dividing up some of the larger clusters.

▶

7 Starting at the bottom of the obelisks, push in the roses horizontally, using firm pressure and carefully holding the rose heads, which might otherwise snap off. An easy way to get a perfectly balanced tree is to look down on the arrangement from directly above to ensure the roses are making an even shape around the circumference.

8 Gradually work up the obelisk, turning the pot around to get an even balance of the two colours. Leave small gaps for the berries to be inserted later. Cut the rose stems shorter as you reach the top of the tree. Push the last roses in vertically at the apex.

9 Gently push the light red hypericum berries into any gaps on the first tree, varying the groups from one or two to several berries.

10 Using the darker berries, insert them in the same way on the other tree.

HERB AND DRIED FRUITS WREATH

Lavender and rosemary provide two of the most popular essential oils used in aromatherapy, and the aromas of both combine well with citrus oils. As the fragrance of the fresh herbs in this wreath begins to fade it can be refreshed with a couple of drops of essential oil.

YOU WILL NEED
rosemary
secateurs (pruners)
blue-dyed raffia
woven twig wreath
dried orange slices
medium-gauge stub wires
lavender
dried poppy seed heads
glue gun and glue sticks

1 Divide the rosemary branches into sprigs approximately 15 cm/6 in long using secateurs (pruners). Tie one end of the raffia to the wreath and bind the rosemary sprigs to the top and sides.

2 Thread two or three slices of dried orange on to a stub wire, leaving enough wire at either end to bind around the wreath. Repeat to make five groups.

3 Using raffia, tie the stems of lavender together in groups of eight to ten to make tiny posies approximately 5 cm/2 in long.

4 Place the orange slices in position and then take the wire around the sides and twist the two ends together at the back of the wreath. The wire will also help to keep the rosemary firmly in place.

5 Position the lavender bunches between the groups of orange slices, making sure the flower heads follow the line of the rosemary sprigs; secure firmly with raffia.

6 Cut the stems off the poppy seed heads, taking care not to puncture the heads, which are probably still full of seeds. Give the base of each seed head a generous blob of hot glue, and immediately press it on to the wreath wherever there is an obvious space around the orange slices or to conceal any wire that may be showing. Turn the wreath around to decide which way up looks best and tie a piece of raffia to the top. Hang the wreath from a picture hook that is securely fixed to the wall as the finished ring is quite heavy.

ROMANTIC BEDSIDE POSY

Hand-tied arrangements of flowers are created in one hand with the other adding stems angled in one direction to create a spiral effect. The finished circular design, with the stems cut to the same length, is ready to go straight into a vase. The tie is left around the flowers to hold the shape.

YOU WILL NEED
scented roses
spray carnations
astrantia
great burnet
sweet cicely
scissors or sharp knife
mirror (optional)
natural raffia
small wide-mouthed vase

1 Separate the flowers into groups and discard any with broken stems.

2 Strip off any flowers or foliage that will eventually be below the binding point. Depending on the desired height of the final bouquet, this point is between one-third and halfway up each stem.

3 Remove any thorns on the roses by carefully trimming them off with scissors or a sharp knife, making sure you do not damage the roses' stems.

4 To start the spiral, hold two or three of the straightest stems together, then add subsequent stems in the same direction at about a 45° angle, turning the bouquet to keep it evenly balanced. ▶

5 Keep turning the bouquet as you add more flowers. You may find it easier to make this arrangement in front of a mirror so you can view all sides.

6 Hold the bouquet so you can see it from above: if there are any spaces they can be filled by relaxing the hand holding the flowers and inserting an additional stem with the other hand.

7 Hold the bouquet horizontally from time to time to make sure there are no gaps.

8 Save the sweet cicely until last so its fronds form a soft collar around the other flowers. Bind a length of raffia around the stems where you were holding the flowers. The raffia needs to be tied firmly but not so tightly that it crushes the stems.

9 Cut all the stems to the same length using a pair of scissors or a sharp knife. Place the tied bouquet in the vase, trimming off more of the stems if necessary.

AL FRESCO FRUIT VASES

The hollowed-out rinds of melon are often used as serving dishes for individual fruit salads, but they also make attractive containers for fresh flowers. You could also use half grapefruits, oranges and lemons, or vegetables such as pumpkins, marrow or even hollowed-out savoy cabbages.

YOU WILL NEED
small watermelon
kitchen knife
spoon
cantaloupe melon
spray chrysanthemums
yellow and orange carthamus (safflower)
flowering dill
pink and mauve sweet peas
chive flowers
ivy-leaved pelargonium flowers
scissors or sharp knife
jug
flower food

1 Cut the watermelon in half and make incisions across the diameter as if cutting a cake. Insert the knife between the flesh and the rind and work it around to release the flesh. Spoon it out carefully and reserve for later use.

2 Very ripe cantaloupe melons have a much softer flesh that can simply be scooped out with a spoon. If the melon does not stand completely flat, then trim a little off the bottom.

3 Divide the flowers into groups and cut individual flower sprays from the chrysanthemums.

4 Fill the halved, hollowed-out melons with water and flower food.

5 Push the stiff stems of carthamus (safflower) into the remaining flesh of the melons to hold them securely around the edge. Add one or two dill flower heads to each melon half to make a framework for the other flowers.

6 Add the spray chrysanthemums, turning the melons to make sure each arrangement is balanced from all sides as it is intended for a table centre.

7 The rest of the flowers should now be able to support the softer stems of the sweet peas and chive flowers, which should be inserted carefully.

8 As a complete clash of colour, add a few stems of pelargonium flowers: use one of the pretty ivy-leaved varieties, which often have bright, bicoloured petals, or a spray of leaves and flowers from a scented pelargonium.

Above: These flower-filled fruit bowls are a perfect decoration for a light summer meal; and you can include the scooped-out fruits in the food you are serving.

TRADITIONAL BOUQUET

Despite the popularity of hand-tied posies ready to go straight into a vase, a flat bouquet is an arrangement still used by many florists. Quite often the flower stems are of varying lengths and are difficult to arrange together, so split the flowers between two or three vases to solve the problem.

YOU WILL NEED
flat bouquet containing standard carnations, spray chrysanthemums, solidago (golden rod), Asian hybrid lilies, roses
scissors or sharp knife
bucket
flower food
garden foliage such as honeysuckle or spiraea
secateurs (pruners)
3 glass vases of varying heights

1 It is quite likely that the bouquet was made up several hours before you received it and the flowers are in need of a long drink. Unwrap the bouquet and unless the stem ends have been covered with damp tissue, snip off the end of each stem, remove all the lower leaves and place the flowers in a bucket deeply filled with cool water and with flower food added.

2 After an hour or so any of the flowers that were slightly wilted should have revived. Lay out the flowers on the cellophane and divide them into groups of the same variety.

3 Select some foliage from the garden to make more of the flowers. Cut branches using secateurs (pruners) and making a clean incision. Never crush woody stems with a hammer as it impedes their ability to take up water.

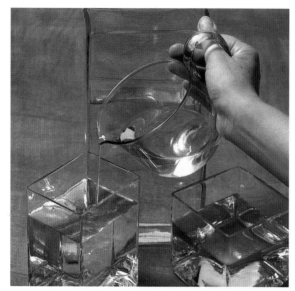

4 Make sure all the vases are scrupulously clean and fill with water and flower food.

5 As the lilies and solidago (golden rod) have stems of similar lengths, arrange them together. Remove any leaves that will fall below the water line and add some green foliage from your garden selection.

6 With odd-length carnations, cut them all to the same length. Cut all the individual sprays from the chrysanthemums and arrange in your hand to make a tight posy. With all the leaves removed, carnations and chrysanthemums may last for about 3 weeks in a cool room.

7 Even florist's roses can be persuaded to look like garden blooms if combined with some cottage-garden foliage such as honeysuckle. To improve their longevity, make sure all the leaves that will fall below the water line are removed.

EXOTIC FLOWERS

Exotics such as protea have tough, woody stems and heavy flower heads. Their bold architectural quality can be overpowering, and they need other strong shapes to keep a harmonious balance. Celosia, curcuma and amaranthus make this an arrangement that could be from a tropical paradise.

YOU WILL NEED
statice stems
scissors or secateurs (pruners)
Celosia argentea var. cristata
sturdy glass vase, preferably reflecting
the colours of the flowers
jug
flower food
curcuma
Protea cynaroides
exotic leaves
Amaranthus caudatus 'Viridis'

1 Exotic leaves are an appropriate foliage, but the leaves of statice have a cactus-like quality that complements the tropical flowers. Trim off any of the statice leaves that may fall below the water line.

2 Remove all the leaves from the celosia as they often conceal the lower flowers. Make sure no leaves or leaf axils remain on the stems, but try to avoid damaging the stems when trimming them as this may affect the flowers' longevity.

3 Fill the vase with fresh water and flower food and insert enough stems of statice to create a network of foliage to support the heavy flower heads.

4 Place the celosia in between the foliage, cutting the stems at various different lengths to create different heights in the vase.

5 Add the curcuma, cutting their stems at different heights to keep all the flowers clearly visible.

6 By now there is a strong enough support system in the vase to carry the weight of the protea. Leave enough space around the flower heads to allow their petals to open.

7 Add a few exotic leaves to the arrangement to provide a foil for the flowers.

8 Very gently insert the stems of amaranthus around the edge of the vase so the tassel-like flowers can dangle over the edge.

GOLDEN WALNUT POTS

Gilt cream transforms a humble terracotta pot into a golden vase for special occasions, especially for Christmas. Old, weathered pots work best as their rough texture gives an attractive broken colour effect. Gilded walnuts nestle between creamy spray chrysanthemums and sprays of alstroemeria.

YOU WILL NEED
rubber gloves
paintbrush
gilt cream paint
small terracotta flowerpot
plastic sheet or small plastic bag
scissors or sharp knife
adhesive tape
walnuts
stub wires
small and medium-sized ivy leaves
florist's foam sphere
flower food
spray chrysanthemums
pointed stick or skewer
alstroemeria (Peruvian lilies)
roses

1 Wearing rubber gloves, brush a little gilt cream paint on to the sides of the terracotta pot.

2 Rub the cream in using your fingers. You need only a tiny amount of gilt cream to create a soft golden glow.

3 Line the pot with a sheet of plastic or a small plastic bag. Trim the edges and stick them down using adhesive tape.

4 Cover each walnut with a layer of gilt cream. Used very sparingly, the cream will dry in a couple of minutes. Taking a piece of wire, push the end up into the centre of the nut. If the nuts are fresh, the juicy kernel inside will hold the wire firmly.

5 Select a couple of ivy leaves and thread them on to the wire at the base of each leaf, trimming off any remaining stem.

6 Select four or five larger ivy leaves and place them around the edge of the pot so each leaf is about halfway across the rim.

7 Soak the foam sphere in deep water with flower food added and hold under the surface until the air bubbles stop rising to the surface. Press the foam into the pot until it feels firm. The ivy leaves will form a green collar. ▶

8 Push the wired walnuts into the foam, leaving spaces between them for the flowers. Make sure they are regularly spaced around the whole sphere.

9 Cut off individual flower sprays from the chrysanthemums, removing any leaves or leaf axils. The smoother the stems the easier it is to push them into the foam. Make a hole in the foam using a pointed stick or skewer and then insert the flower.

10 Add the alstroemeria (Peruvian lilies) in the same way as the chrysanthemums. Alstroemeria have quite soft stems so it is essential to make a hole for each flower before pressing it into the foam.

11 Finally, add the roses, having removed all the leaves and thorns.

AROMATIC CHRISTMAS WREATH

Huge, luxurious blooms like this deep red 'Preference' rose, blended with the aromatic oils of cedarwood, frankincense and myrrh, will scent your home evocatively at Christmas. Pure rose essential oil is very expensive, but a rose-scented synthetic oil is an acceptable alternative here.

YOU WILL NEED
omorica cones (or very small pine cones)
plastic bag
suggested mixture of oils: 40 drops
synthetic rose-scented oil, 20 drops
cedarwood, 20 drops frankincense,
20 drops myrrh
florist's foam wreath with integral
plastic tray
flower food
3 claret-coloured candles
stub wires
artificial red berries
fresh holly sprigs
secateurs (pruners)
pointed stick or skewer
large-headed red roses

1 Put the omorica cones into a plastic bag. Mix the oils, add them to the bag and shake well for a few minutes. If possible, do this step 3–4 days before assembling the wreath to give the cones time to absorb the oils.

2 Soak the foam wreath in fresh water with flower food added until the maximum amount of water has been absorbed. Position the candles at regular intervals around the wreath, pressing them down to the base of the foam.

3 Wind the end of a stub wire around the base of each scented cone, pulling it firmly so the wire is hardly visible.

▶

4 Holly rarely grows berries where you want them and they perish very quickly. Artificial alternatives combined with real leaves look very convincing and last all through Christmas. Wire them together in small bunches, leaving the wire ends long enough to press into the foam.

5 Be careful handling holly as the leaves are very sharp; you may feel more comfortable using gardening gloves. Cut off small twigs with the brightest leaves and, making a small hole in the foam, press each one in gently. Cover both the inner and outer sides of the foam as well as the top.

6 Add the wired artificial berries towards the centre of a group of leaves to make them look more authentic. Just a few bunches is enough – any more and every-one will know that they are fake.

7 Cut the rose stems to about 7.5 cm/3 in, to allow the heads to sit above the holly and give them space for the petals to open. Make a hole before inserting each rose. It is likely that the arrangement will be placed in a warm room, but you can prolong its life by taking the roses out at night and placing them somewhere cool in a small container of water and flower food.

8 Add the cones, which will exude a rich floral and spicy aroma that will fill the room.

FLOWER EGGS

Eggs are synonymous with Easter, but these flower-filled eggs are decorative at any time of year and this is a lovely project for children to do with any small flowers. White or very pale brown eggs take up the dye or food colouring most successfully; you could also use duck or goose eggs.

YOU WILL NEED
white or pale-shelled hens' eggs
sharp skewer or sharp-pointed knife
bowl
glass tumbler (water glass) or jar for
dyeing each egg
food colouring or fabric dye
rubber gloves
egg cups or small shot glasses
jug
flower food
chive leaves and chive flower heads
lady's mantle (*Alchemilla mollis*)
small campanula
zinnia
scissors or sharp knife

1 Make a small hole in the top of each egg using a skewer or the tip of a sharp knife. Carefully peel away enough of the shell to allow the contents to escape easily. Empty the eggs into a bowl for use later. Wash out each shell thoroughly.

2 Pour water into several glass tumblers (water glasses) or jars, each big enough to hold one egg comfortably. Add a tiny amount of food colouring or fabric dye, a different colour for each glass, and mix well. Using rubber gloves to protect your hands, gently put an eggshell in each glass, making sure that it is completely immersed. The shells will take up the colour in a few minutes and the stronger the solution the more intense the colour of the egg. ▶

3 Remove the eggshells from the dye and allow to dry. Place in egg cups or small glasses and fill with water and flower food. Choose a variety of small-headed seasonal flowers that are appropriately coloured to go with the tones you have dyed the eggs.

4 Cut the flowers to length so they are no taller than twice the height of the egg. Arrange them very carefully in the shells, peeling away some of the shell if the hole in the top is too small.

5 It doesn't matter if the edge of the hole is jagged and uneven as this will be concealed once the flowers are inserted.

SPRING FLOWER BASKET

A wooden trug is ideal for a wide, shallow arrangement, especially if placed on a low table to be seen from above, and a brimming basket of spring flowers would make a lovely Mother's Day present. For an Easter gift the mossy "nest" could be filled with tiny gold-covered chocolate eggs.

YOU WILL NEED
wooden trug
strong plastic sheet
6 tacks or drawing pins
hammer
scissors or sharp knife
double-sided tape
2 glass jars
2 blocks of florist's foam
jug
flower food
'Apricot Beauty' tulips
ranunculus
lily of the valley
two handfuls of carpet moss (sheet moss)
honeysuckle
medium-gauge stub wires
wire cutters
kumquats
handful of glass pebbles

1 Line the trug with plastic, fixing it around the edges with tacks. Trim the overhanging plastic with scissors.

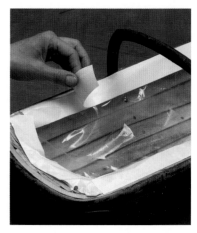

2 Stick double-sided tape all around the inner edge of the trug, following the curves and trimming where necessary. This provides a tacky edge that the moss can stick to so that it will conceal the plastic.

3 Place the two jars in the trug and keep them secure by wedging them with florist's foam that has been soaked in water with flower food added. The foam will provide a moist base to keep the moss green and fresh. Fill the jars with water and flower food.

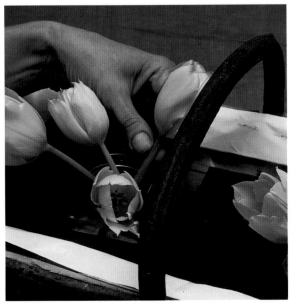

4 Cut the stems of the tulips to about 15 cm/6 in. Remove any leaves and place an equal number of tulips in each jar.

5 Repeat with the ranunculus to create a rounded posy shape in each jar. Turn the basket to make sure the flowers are balanced on both sides.

6 Cut the lily of the valley stems slightly longer than the tulips and ranunculus, so they just rise above the the others, and retain the leaves.

7 Carefully cover all the florist's foam and double-sided tape with moss, creating a shallow "nest" between the jars of flowers.

8 Add the honeysuckle, allowing it trail over the moss. Leave space for the kumquats.

9 Cut stub wires into 5 cm/2 in lengths using wire cutters and insert a piece of wire through the base of each kumquat.

10 Bend the wire ends down and push them into the florist's foam to make two small clusters of kumquats in the corners of the basket.

11 Fill the "nest" with a couple of handfuls of glass pebbles. This arrangement will keep fresh for several days, but may need gentle moistening with a water spray. As individual flowers fade they can easily be replaced with fresh ones, and by doing this you could keep the arrangement for several weeks.

SPRING FLOWERS

Narrow glass tanks offer the possibility of a graphic style that complements many modern interiors. While flowers are the stars of any composition, luscious green stems can be an attractive feature in transparent containers, particularly the perfect, straight stalks of many spring bulb varieties.

YOU WILL NEED
3 glass tanks, one slightly taller than
the other two
jug
flower food
'Monte Carlo' tulips
scissors or sharp knife
clear water-resistant adhesive tape
chincherinchee
allium moly

1 Make sure the tanks are sparkling and thoroughly clean inside and out and fill with water and flower food. Sort the flowers.

2 Trim and clean the stems very carefully, removing any dirt or loose leaves that will sink to the bottom of the vase and pollute and discolour the water.

3 Cut one tulip to a length such that the top of the stem is level with the top of the tallest vase. Use this flower as a template to cut all the other tulips.

4 Arrange the tulips in the tank so that each stem is completely upright.

5 Stick a piece of water-resistant adhesive tape across the centre of the smaller tanks as the allium and chincherinchee flower heads are smaller and you will need to make two rows of flowers.

6 Cut the stems of chincherinchee in the same way as the tulips and fill one tank with two rows of these flowers, making each stalk stand upright.

7 Repeat the process with the allium to fill the remaining tank.

TULIPS AND EUPHORBIA

Wide-mouthed vases give the most scope and flexibility when arranging flowers but the stems need support. Chicken wire would look ugly in a glass vase, but bare twigs such as pussy willow or contorted willow can be used instead to create a natural, attractive framework.

YOU WILL NEED
wide-mouthed glass vase
jug
flower food
secateurs (pruners)
pussy willow
euphorbia
rubber gloves
matches
'Moncella' tulips

1 Fill the vase with water and flower food. Using secateurs (pruners), cut the willow twigs so that they will come just above the top of the vase.

2 Arrange the willow so that the twigs make a criss-cross network that will provide support for the other flowers.

3 The sap from euphorbia can cause skin irritations, and it is best to handle the stems using rubber gloves. Strip off all the lower leaves and cut to size.

4 To prevent the sap leaching out and possibly reducing the life of the other flowers, carefully singe each cut euphorbia stem with a lighted match. ▶

5 Add the euphorbia to the vase, turning the vase
   as you do so to make sure the arrangement is
balanced on all sides.

6 Finally, add the tulips. These will now be
   supported by the pussy willow and euphorbia,
making it easy to place the flowers exactly where you
want them in the arrangement.

FRAGRANT POSIES

A tiny posy makes the perfect gift for many occasions: a handful of sensitively chosen flowers can say "Thank you", "Happy birthday" or "I love you". Garden flowers are very special, but bought flowers can be personalized by adding some leaves and wrapping the posy beautifully.

YOU WILL NEED

a) garden pinks, Spanish sage (*Salvia lavandulifolia*), everlasting pea (*Lathyrus sylvestris*), red clover

b) lavender, pink roses, orange carthamus (safflower), thyme, alpine strawberry leaves

c) pink roses, pink lacecap hydrangea, eryngium (sea holly)

d) horsemint (*Mentha longifolia*), blue cornflowers, lady's mantle (*Alchemilla mollis*), soapwort seed pods (*Saponaria officinalis*)

scissors or sharp knife

natural raffia

ribbon

coloured tissue paper

clear cellophane

clear adhesive tape

pin

1 To make a posy, assemble all the flowers into individual groups. Trim off all the lower leaves that are likely to fall below the water line when the posy is put into a vase.

2 Arrange the flowers in one hand, adding additional flowers with the other hand while turning the growing bunch, until you have a rounded and balanced posy. Wrap a piece of natural raffia around the stems several times to hold the flowers. Lay the posy on its side and tie the raffia firmly but not so tightly it squashes the stalks. Trim the stems to the same length.

3 If you have some suitable large leaves, you can make a posy with a protective frill around it. Lay out the flowers and prepare the stems as before.

4 Assemble the posy and, before tying it, add a "collar" of flat leaves such as these strawberry leaves. Tie with raffia and trim the stems. ▶

5 If you are making a posy that needs to be carried, you can bind the stems into a handle using ribbon. Tie the finished posy with raffia first.

6 Take a piece of ribbon approximately twice the height of the posy and, leaving enough at one end to tie a bow, wind the ribbon from the binding point, overlapping each twist to conceal the raffia and the stems. When you reach the bottom, tuck the ribbon over the base of the stems and then wind it back up.

7 When you reach the top of the stems, tie the ribbon in a knot to prevent it from unravelling and then tie a bow, cutting the ribbon ends on a slant to stop them fraying.

8 For a posy that needs to travel and yet still arrive fresh, you need to cover it to protect the flowers and also to help prevent evaporation. For long journeys, it is also wise to wrap some wet tissue or cotton wool around the stem ends. Prepare the flowers as before.

9 Make up the posy and tie with raffia. Cut two squares of tissue paper approximately twice the size of the posy. Cut a square piece of clear cellophane about 10 cm/4 in wider and longer than the tissue.

10 Lay the two pieces of tissue wrong side up, with the top piece at 45° to the other. Lay the cellophane on top: this will provide a waterproof layer between the flowers and the tissue and also prevent excess evaporation. Place the posy on its side and wrap the paper in folds around it as you roll it from one corner diagonally to the opposite one.

11 Fasten the paper around the stems with raffia, ribbon or clear adhesive tape. There should be enough cellophane at the top to pin together over the flowers to keep them from drying out.

Above: These gift posies provide a ready-arranged bouquet that can simply be untied and placed in a vase.

TECHNIQUES

Arranging fresh flowers in a natural and contemporary style requires very few techniques. All the arrangements in this book are created in a few minutes. Their elegant simplicity is achieved by choosing the flowers carefully and selecting containers that complement the design.

FLORIST'S FOAM

1 Add flower food to the water, then soak the foam until all the air bubbles have stopped rising to the surface – this usually takes 1-2 minutes depending on the size of the foam. Don't leave it soaking any longer or it will disintegrate.

2 If you need a very small piece of foam, cut it off a dry block. Once the foam is soaked it loses its effectiveness if dried and soaked again. However, it is much easier to cut the foam to shape once it is thoroughly wet.

3 Many flower stems are quite fragile and it is best to make a hole in the foam with a sharp stick or skewer. Even rigid stems benefit as pushing them into the foam can inhibit their ability to take up water and reduce their longevity.

WIRING WALNUTS

WIRING KUMQUATS

WIRING OMORICA CONES

Small fruits or nuts need a florist's wire with good rigidity. A 90 mm gauge will provide enough support. To wire a walnut, push the wire between the two halves of the shell and through to the inside of the top to lodge firmly in the flesh.

To wire kumquats, push a 10 cm/4 in length of 90 mm wire through the base of the fruit. Repeat with another piece of wire at right angles to the first, then bend the ends down and twist them, making a strong support.

These delightful little cones are often used in potpourri and are more delicate than pine cones. Using a fine 71 mm wire, wind a 10 cm/4 in piece around the lower tier of the cone and continue until it is firmly attached.

REMOVING LOWER LEAVES

Before arranging flowers, always trim the ends of their stems, making a long diagonal cut with a sharp knife or scissors. Remove any foliage that will fall below the water level in the vase. Unless roses are being arranged in a hand-held posy, it is unnecessary to remove the thorns.

REVIVING FLOWERS

1 It is usually possible to revive wilted flowers by cutting a generous piece off the bottom of each stem. This should be at least 10 cm/4 in; more is better. This part of the stem has usually dried out and is unable to take up water. The flowers may also have been infected by bacteria, which block up the delicate cells in the stems.

2 Once the stems have been cut and most of the foliage removed, a long cool drink in a deep container of fresh tepid water with added flower food will revive most flowers. If possible, fill the container so the level of the water is just below the flower heads.

FLOWER FOOD

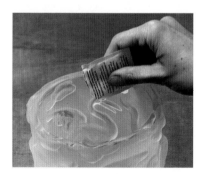

Always add flower food to the vase water. It encourages buds to open, and inhibits the growth of bacteria in the water, which could cause the flowers to wilt and die prematurely. Don't change the vase water once flower food has been added, just top up when required.

SINGEING STEMS

Euphorbia stems secrete a white milky sap that may cause skin irritations for some people and can also weaken other flowers in an arrangement. This can be prevented by gently singeing the end of the cut stem with a lighted taper or match.

PLUGGING STEMS

Some flowers, such as delphinium and hippeastrum, are top-heavy and prone to keeling over. This can be avoided by gently inserting a thin cane or stick up the centre of each hollow stem, which allows them to take up water and keeps the stems firm and rigid.

MATERIALS AND EQUIPMENT

For many arrangements, little is needed beyond a good pair of sharp scissors, but on special occasions you may plan more elaborate displays that need more support.

RAFFIA

Natural raffia is ideal for tying flowers together as it is strong but does not bite into the stems. Coloured raffia is perfect for making lush trailing bows.

CARPET MOSS (SHEET MOSS)

This moss is useful for covering the surface of arrangements to conceal individual containers, creating the illusion that the flowers are growing in the basket or container.

CELLOPHANE

Use cellophane for wrapping bouquets, as a waterproof lining for porous containers and scrunched up as an invisible support for stems in a vase.

GILT CREAM PAINT

This decorative cream gives a sheen to nuts, cones and fruits as well as containers such as terracotta pots. It is available in gold, silver and bronze.

PEBBLES AND SHELLS

Pebbles and shells make a decorative mulch and an attractive support for flower stems in glass vases.

GLASS STONES

Polished glass stones are widely available from gift shops and garden centres, where there is a wide range of colours to choose from. The transparent ones are most versatile as they resemble precious crystals in the bottom of a glass vase or bowl.

FLOATING CANDLES

Candlelight is as flattering for fresh flowers as it is for faces. A bowl of floating candles surrounded by beautiful fragrant flowers makes a stunning table centrepiece. Never leave lit candles unattended and make sure they are extinguished before leaving a room.

GLUE GUN AND GLUE STICKS

This electrically powered tool melts sticks of glue that ooze from its nozzle activated by a trigger. It is a dream machine for instantly attaching fresh and dried flowers to containers, wreaths, headdresses and garlands. The liquid glue is extremely hot and potentially dangerous if left unattended and should be kept out of reach of children.

ADHESIVE TAPES

Waterproof adhesive tape is useful for sticking plastic or cellophane to the inside of containers. Strong adhesive double-sided tape provides a removable surface on which to stick decorative materials such as moss or vegetables to the sides of vases and containers.

NUTS AND CONES

Walnuts, hazelnuts, acorns and all types of cones can be combined with fresh flowers, especially in those arrangements designed for autumn and Christmas. It is sometimes appropriate to add a sheen of gold or silver using gilt cream paint.

CANES AND FLORIST'S WIRE

Thin canes can be used to support hollow and top-heavy stems. Florist's wires are useful for making false stems to fix cones and nuts to fresh flower designs.

FLORIST'S SCISSORS

The most important piece of equipment that no flower arranger can afford to be without is a pair of strong and very sharp scissors. There are numerous designs for both left- and right-handed flower arrangers. Making a clean, diagonal slant cut on flower stems minimizes the damage to their delicate cell tissue and allows them to take up the maximum amount of water.

FLOWER FOOD

The correct amount of flower food should be used in every vase. This harmless preparation of mild disinfectant and sugar inhibits growth of bacteria in the water and encourages buds to mature and open.

SECATEURS (PRUNERS)

Secateurs (pruners) are more practical than scissors for cutting wires and tough branches.

Above: raffia (1); carpet moss (sheet moss) (2); cellophane (3); gilt cream (4); pebbles and shells (5); glass stones (6); floating candles (7); glue gun (8); adhesive tapes (9); nuts and cones (10); canes and florist's wire (11); florist's scissors (12); flower food (13); secateurs (pruners) (14).

CONTAINERS

A vase is important to a floral design, but the flowers are the stars. However, the type of container you choose should complement the flowers you are arranging.

FLORIST'S FOAM

As well as the familiar brick shape, spheres and rings are also available, all in various sizes. Spheres may be covered with flowers and hung from ribbon to make bridesmaids' posies. The rings have a built-in plastic drip tray; filled with flowers, they make table centrepieces that look very effective when surrounding a dish of floating candles.

BASKETS

Shallow baskets lined with plastic and filled with florist's foam concealed with moss provide a support for flowers, and deeper baskets can hide several containers filled with fresh blooms. Light plywood baskets can be painted with a water-based emulsion.

GLASS TANKS

These vases are immensely versatile and are effective used singly or in a group of varying heights. They can be used to contain a mass of flowers or just a few stems that can be supported by filling the tanks with glass pebbles or stones.

GLASSES AND JARS

Simple, straight-sided drinking glasses are cheap and perfect for small posies and table centrepieces. Larger glass pots combined with smaller inner glass jam jars or vases provide a gap that can be filled with shells, pebbles or fragrant potpourri. Tiny shot glasses or egg cups make ideal vases for individual table-setting arrangements.

TERRACOTTA POTS

Natural coloured terracotta pots complement country-style arrangements, and with a simple wash of diluted emulsion paint they can be gently coloured in minutes to suit any number of styles. As terracotta is porous, the pots need to be used with an inner container or lined with plastic if using florist's foam.

METAL CONTAINERS

Some metals react with water and can cause flowers to die prematurely and obviously shouldn't be used, but galvanized metal is safe and rustproof. A tall metal bucket is ideal for supporting the height of long stems or large branches of foliage, and you can minimize the weight by using a smaller inner container that helps to keep the stems in place.

Right: florist's foam (1); baskets (2); glass tanks (3); glasses and jars (4); terracotta pots (5); metal containers (6).

FLOWER CARE AND CONDITIONING

Whether you are picking a posy from the garden or choosing some blooms from a local florist or supermarket, it is important that you can recognize flowers in their peak condition. And once you have purchased your flowers, there are a number of things you can do to make sure you get the best from them for as long as possible.

Most flowers should be picked or purchased when they are in bud with several coloured petals showing. If they are spike-shaped flowers like eremurus (foxtail lily) or delphinium, make sure some of the lower florets are open. Flowers such as narcissi and particularly daffodils may be picked or bought in tight green bud as they open very quickly when placed in water. Conversely, gerbera (Transvaal daisies) and chrysanthemums are both sold fully open, but these flowers can still last for at least two weeks. Always check to see that none of the petals have brown edges, which indicates that the flowers are well past their sell-by date, and ensure that the leaves are green and healthy with no traces of brown.

Do not leave flowers out of water as the stem ends dry out very quickly. If you have to transport them, cover the stem ends with damp tissue or newspaper and wrap the flowers in paper or cellophane to avoid excess evaporation, which causes the flowers to wilt.

If you are taking flowers from the garden, pick them in the cool of the morning or evening and place them in water straight away.

Always trim the ends of flower stems before arranging them, making a long, clean diagonal cut with a sharp knife or scissors. This provides the maximum surface for the flowers to take up water and means they are less likely to wilt. Even woody stems must be cut in

Left: Grow perennial herbs like thyme and sage, evergreen climbers and trailing plants to provide a constant source of foliage for creating natural shapes and support for both garden and shop-bought flowers.

Right: (clockwise) Blue delphinium, eryngium (sea holly), nigella (love-in-a-mist) and cornflowers are country-garden flowers that can all be dried very successfully.

the same way: if necessary, use a pair of sharp secateurs (pruners). Never crush stems with a hammer as this damages the delicate cell structure in the stem and allows bacteria to develop, which prevents the flowers or foliage taking up water. Before arranging, all flowers appreciate a long, cool drink in deep water for as long as possible, preferably overnight.

Before arranging the flowers, remove any foliage that will be submerged in the vase. Leaves that remain underwater start to rot very quickly, and the bacteria that are produced from this process not only block the flower stems but also makes the water green and smelly and unpleasant to look at.

Make sure all your vases and containers are completely clean before you use them. Use fresh, tepid water as this contains the least amount of air. If air bubbles get into the stems they can cause a blockage, restricting the flow of water and causing wilting, or in the case of roses, drooping flower heads.

Always add flower food to the water. It contains the right amount of sugar needed to encourage buds to open, and a mild disinfectant that inhibits the growth of the bacteria that cause flower heads to droop and foliage to wilt prematurely. Homemade remedies such as aspirin, household bleach and lemonade do work sometimes, but it is a very hit-and-miss solution as it is vital to get the exact balance of sugar and disinfectant. Years of scientific research have made the commercial flower food products consistently safe and successful. Most flower sellers provide a sachet with every purchase.

Opposite: Commercially grown roses vary in price depending on the size of the flower head and length of the stem. It is best to buy roses a couple of days before a special occasion to allow them to open.

Left: Coordinated colour designs need flowers of different shapes to give impact and definition, such as spike-shaped chincherinchee and allium with oval-shaped tulips, or rosette-shaped ranunculus contrasted with the more delicate and leafy lady's mantle (Alchemilla mollis).

Right: Spray chrysanthemums are one of the longest-lasting cut flowers, and their leaves fade long before the flowers. For more contemporary-looking arrangements, cut them short, remove most of the foliage and combine them with other bright, strong colours like carthamus (safflower) and calendula (pot marigolds).

Left: Pink astrantia and white phlox are delicate flowers that combine perfectly with the tall spikes of moluccella (bells of Ireland). The white flowers are insignificant but its soft green bell-shaped calyces give shape to an arrangement.

Keep flowers in a cool and well-ventilated atmosphere that is well away from icy draughts or hot fires in winter and direct sunlight in summer. The ethylene gas that is produced by mature fruit and vegetables is detrimental to flowers as it speeds up the ripening process. Ethylene is quite harmless and useful if you want to ripen green tomatoes – place them with fully mature apples – but make sure you keep the fruit away from your flowers.

Check your flower vases regularly and top them up with water in hot weather as it evaporates more quickly in high temperatures. When you use flower food, it is unnecessary to change the water. Remove any dying flowers and leaves as these faded blooms may affect the longevity of other flowers in the vase.

COLOURS

YELLOWS AND ORANGES
Alstroemeria (Peruvian lily)
Calendula (pot marigold)
Chrysanthemum
Dianthus (carnation)
Freesia
Gerbera
Gloriosa (glory vine)
Lilium (lily)
Narcissus (daffodil)
Papaver (poppy)
Physalis (Chinese lantern)
Ranunculus (turban
 buttercup)
Rosa (rose)
Tulipa (tulip)

Freesia
Gerbera
Gladiolus (gladioli)
Hippeastrum (amaryllis)
Lathyrus (sweet pea)
Rosa (rose)
Tulipa (tulip)
Zinnia

PINKS
Allium (onion flower)
Astrantia (masterwort)
Campanula (bellflower)
Delphinium
Dianthus (carnation)
Freesia
Hydrangea
Lavatera (mallow)
Nigella (love-in-a-mist)
Paeonia (peony)
Phlox

REDS
Alstroemeria (Peruvian lily)
Anemone
Astilbe

PURPLES AND BLUES
Allium (onion flower)
Anemone
Campanula (bellflower)
Centaurea (cornflower)
Delphinium
Echinops (globe thistle)
Freesia
Hyacinthus (hyacinth)
Iris
Lavandula (lavender)
Limonium (statice)
Lisianthus (eustoma)
Nigella (love-in-a-mist)
Veronica

GREEN
Alchemilla (lady's mantle)
Amaranthus (tassle flower)
Anethum (dill)
Euphorbia (spurge)

Helichrysum (everlasting
 flower)
Moluccella (bells of Ireland)

WHITE
Anemone
Campanula (bellflower)
Chrysanthemum
Convallaria (lily of
 the valley)
Delphinium
Freesia
Gardenia
Iris
Lathyrus (sweet pea)
Lisianthus (eustoma)
Nigella (love-in-a-mist)
Ranunculus (turban
 buttercup)
Rosa (rose)
Tulipa (tulip)

ACKNOWLEDGMENTS
The author and publishers would like to thank Rosemary Titterington at Iden Croft Herbs, Bill Le Grice in Norfolk for his spectacular roses on p. 24, Damask in London for their lace and quilts on p. 36 and p. 44, Chris Johnson at Sia Parlane for all the glass vases and Heather Clarke at Gastronomic Adventures for the delicious food. And very special thanks to Michelle Garrett and Dulcie, and last but not least, Tony Flavin, who is a very special flower person.

INDEX

al fresco fruit vases, 50-3
alliums, 74-76, 93
alstroemeria, 60-3
amaranthus, 57-9
asparagus, 16-19
astrantia, 16-19, 47-9, 94

basket, spring flower, 70-3
bouquet, traditional, 54-6

calendulas, 20-2
candles, 26-8, 64-6, 86-7
carnations, 26-8, 47-9,
    54-6
carthamus, 50-3
cellophane, 32-5
celosia, 57-9
chillies, 26-8
chincherinchee, 74-6, 93
Christmas wreath, aromatic,
    64-6
chrysanthemums, 29-31, 50-1,
    54-6, 60-62, 94
cinnamon sticks, 21
colours, 95
conditioning flowers, 90-4
containers, 88-9
cornflowers, 12-15, 80-3, 91
courgette flowers, 20-2
curcuma, 57-60

delphiniums, 36-9, 85, 91
dill, 36-9, 50-3

edible flowers, 20-2
eggs, flower, 67-9
equipment, 86-7
euphorbia, 77-9, 85
exotic flowers, 57-9

ferns, 36-9
flower food, 85, 87

gerbera, 26-8
gloriosa, 10-11

herbs, 23-5, 44-6, 90
holly, 64-6
honeysuckle, 70-3
horsemint, 16-19, 80-3
hypericum berries, 40-3

ivy, 60-3

jasmine, 23-5

kumquats, 70-3, 84

lavender, 44-6, 80-3
lemon balm, 16-19
lilies, 8-11, 32-5, 54-6, 60-2
lily of the valley, 70-3

materials, 86-7
melons, 50-4
molucella, 16-19, 94
mussel shells, 12-15

nigella, 12-15, 90-1

omorica cones, 64-6, 84
onion seed heads, 29-31

pelargoniums, 20-2, 50-53
peonies, 36-9
poppies, 10-11
poppy seed heads, 29-31, 44-6
posies, 47-9, 80-3
pot-et-fleur, scented, 36-9
proteas, 57-9

ranunculus, 70-3, 93
rosemary, 44-6
roses, 20-5, 32-5, 40-3, 47-9, 54-6,
    60-3, 64-6, 80-3, 93

scabious, 12-15
scented flowerpot, 8-11
sea holly, 12-14, 80-3, 90
seaside flowers, 12-15
solidago, 54-6
spring flowers, 70-3, 74-6
'Stargazer' lilies, 8-11
statice, 26-8, 57-9
strawberries, alpine, 16-19
sweet cicely, 47-9
sweet peas, 10-11, 50-3

thistles, alpine, 36-7
topiary tree, three-tier, 29-31
translucent flowers, 32-5
tulips, 70-3, 75-6, 77-9, 93

vegetable vases, summer, 16-19

walnuts, 60-3, 84
wreaths, 26-8, 44-6, 64-6

zinnia, 26-8